I0485710

Designed and Written by Dave Conrey

www.daveconrey.com

Edited by Michele Truty

www.micheletruty.com

Author Photography by Misha Hettie

www.mishahettie.com

ISBN-13: 978-1517318338

ISBN-10: 1517318335

CREATIVE
BADASS
Challenge

Dedicated to my teachers for showing me the path.

And to all the creative souls who might find the path through me.

CREATIVE BADASS Challenge

ONE MONTH TO CHANGE THE WAY YOU LIVE & WORK

by
Dave Conrey

Contents

Preface

As I write this portion of the workbook, ironically the last thing written, it is my two-year anniversary of being laid off from my day job as a magazine art director. The day that happened, I started my full-time journey as an entrepreneur, and I have not looked back.

Through my adventures over the past couple of years, I realized there are three fundamental areas where I've spent the most time working, and they're not what you may assume. When I started my business, I thought tweaking the details of my website, and generating quality content would be the most time-consuming part of my new career, but that was small potatoes compared to other aspects.

Within the Creative Badass Challenge, you're not going to find tips on which marketplace to host your products. You're not going to find out which company is the best place to host your own site. There is no information about which is the best social media platform. In the grand scheme of your creative life, these things are tiny in comparison to the real concerns.

The answers to those items above will always be in a state of flux. Where you sell will likely change in the next eighteen months, and what social sites you use will definitely change by then. Instead of focusing on the unstable aspects, let's talk about the more critical aspects that will always be a factor with you and your work.

The three fundamental areas of your business exist not online, but within you, and they are your emotional, mental, and physical abilities. Within each area, there are details to examine, but let's break down the basics.

Your emotions play a big part in how you show up to life. Your fears, experiences, and behavior dictate a lot of how you act and react to situations. Within the scope of the challenge, I talk often about what to do when you find yourself in emotional situations that may help or hinder your life.

Often our brain gets in the way of progress, whether that's from complete shutdown and burnout, or from overstimulation. Focusing on the important tasks at hand will become a habit for you once you know what to look for.

Finally, what you do with all this information once you have it is critical. The action you take can make or break you, depending on how you handle it. As creatives, we all have passions and big ideas, but what do all those things matter if we don't act upon them? I stress putting in the effort often throughout this challenge, but it's more than just saying, "do the work."

The goal of the Challenge is to equip you with the necessary tools to navigate over and around the various obstacles in your personal and professional life. This is about building up armor against the slings and arrows, but knowing when to lay down the shield if a more open and authentic approach is required.

The original concept for the Challenge was for you to do one challenge a day, as you received them via email. Since this is a book, and nobody is stationed at each chapter to stop you from moving forward, there are no rules to how you progress, as long as you do the challenges as they come. If you want to blaze through this project in a weekend, be my guest, but make sure you put the work in. We will be grading homework. (Not really, but pretend we will.) There would be no point for you to move through a book of challenges if you didn't do any of the actual challenges.

Also, there is a short video to support each day's topic. I link to each video within the individual days, and a page in the back of the workbook with links to each video. I've also included audio versions for those who prefer ears to eyeballs. There are some other bonuses in the back for being generally badass, but I'll let you find them on your own.

One last thing and I'll let you get to work if you happen to stumble or have questions at any time, feel free to email me: dave@freshrag.com. I'll do my best to get back to you in a timely fashion…but I may be working. No, honestly, I'm pretty good about writing back. I hope you enjoy our time together, and I want to support you any way I can.

See you on the inside.

Dave Conrey

The Pregame Show

YOU ARE AFRAID!

You're a quivering scaredy-cat, cowering under the glare of a big dog called life. It's OK, so am I.

The funny thing about fear is that much of what scares us is an illusion. Barring any major psychological phobias, like heights, spiders, or clowns (those dudes are creepy in any scenario), the fears that keep us from achieving greatness in our lives are figments of our own imagination. These fears were ingrained in us over years and years of being beat down by a system that didn't appreciate our creative prowess. That said, just because we've been told throughout our lives that our success is limited, that does not make the claim true.

We all have some perception regarding the limitations of the human experience. Some might believe only a select few have the skill and talent to achieve true greatness in their lives, but truthfully, each and every day, people are breaking records and achieving new things we never thought possible. Back when I was a young punk, skating my degenerate butt all over town, looking for the next hidden half-pipe, it was common knowledge that the 720 (two complete mid-air rotations) was an impossible task. Then another young skate punk by the name of Tony Hawk came on the scene and destroyed that notion. For years, the 720 was the aerial trick of note, and to rotate any further was beyond the limits of human capability. For years, people tried to pull a 900 (2.5 rotations) with nothing but banged knees and the occasional concussion to show for it. Even Tony thought it was impossible, but he never gave up on it.

In 1999, at the ESPN X-Games, at 31 years of age (a relic in terms of skate professionals), Hawk did the impossible. After ten attempts, he pulled off his first 900 aerial. Today, there are only a handful of skaters who can claim to pull off the trick, but more are learning all the time. Because while it's an impressive feat, no doubt, it's not impossible. Every day, records and boundaries are broken by people you don't know, who are changing the way we live our lives. Nobody knew an internal combustion engine was possible before Nikolaus Otto invented it, but now they are in nearly every vehicle, in every driveway, in America and beyond—they are ubiquitous.

Not many people imagined it was possible to go to the moon until President Kennedy made his declaration that it would happen in the following decade. (NASA did it in nine years.) Today, most think planet colonization is impossible, but we cannot know that. To write off a potential future, based only on what we currently know and understand, is foolish and short-sighted.

If you held a gun to my head today and told me to do a handstand or die, I'd be a dead artist. Yet, I saw a video on YouTube in which an Eastern European woman placed her hand on a thin metal stand, and without any momentum, lifted herself completely vertical with nothing but her core arm and body strength. She then spun herself around slowly while performing an acrobatic ballet that blows my mind every time I see it. The important part to remember about this woman is that at some point in her life, she could not do a handstand either.

Human capability is near limitless. The limits we acknowledge now will soon fade into distant memory. The things we cannot do today, and couldn't do before, will become the new normal. I know that I physically cannot do a handstand at this moment, but I also know that if that woman can lift herself into the air as if she was born to do it, then I can eventually do a handstand, if I work at it.

> **DAVE'S NOTE:**
>
> Here's the link to that video:
> www.bit.ly/handbalance

And There's the Rub

Truth: Anybody can achieve greatness.

Also truth: Most will not, because they are not willing to do the work.

This *Creative Badass Challenge* was made to test the limits of what we assume is the normal level of success. You can achieve great things, if you are willing to put yourself 100% into the work. The fact is, though, most people will not do the work needed to make it happen. They will get to certain parts of this challenge and blow them off because they seem frivolous or unnecessary.

Some will skip important details out of haste or fear. They will glaze over aspects of the challenge, because they are not *comfortable* with the task, because it takes them outside their comfort zone. Unfortunately for them, success does not exist within the confines of your comfort zone. Success exists beyond the walls of what you assume is the limit of your capacity for greatness.

This first step is meant to test you. I'm here goading you into action because a certain percentage of you will stop and turn back to your safe hiding place. Others will take the next step and push through the fear. Those who do will find a new world that exists in each new day they push themselves through the challenge. Not only will they expand their circle of comfort with each challenge, but they will learn how to continue to push themselves long after these lessons are done.

The world never stops pushing fear in your face, and the only way to find greatness is to push back, every day, without fail. You cannot stop, ever. Inaction leads to complacency. Complacency leads to inertia, and inertia becomes death to all your big ideas. *That* is moment when you will quit.

Quitting is obviously the exact opposite of success, and since this is not called the Creative Quitting Challenge, it is not what we want from ourselves. Am I right? (That's rhetorical, of course.)

Now, some of you may be wondering how any of this talk about fear, comfort zones, and human capability has anything to do with you selling more stuff. The reason is that if you look at the world's most successful business people, they didn't achieve that level because they knew the right marketing technique or had good branding. It wasn't because they were a people-person or knew how to close a sale. It doesn't even depend on the quality of the products they made (although quality products are definitely a plus). The most successful people became that way because of their beliefs and their unwillingness to accept the status quo.

Steve Jobs, Oprah Winfrey, Richard Branson, and Elon Musk gave status quo the middle finger repeatedly in their lives to get to their level. Now, you may not want to be Steve Jobs or Oprah Winfrey, and that's fine, but there is a level of success you would like to achieve, and it starts with a gesture.

On each day of this challenge, I will leave off with a specific task I want you to perform, an act that will help catapult you past your fear and into the next day. Some days, the act will be straightforward, and on others the act will depend specifically on your circumstances. The important part is that you do the work, because education without action is pointless. The last thing I want is you taking in this information but not applying it. If you are going to be part of this challenge, you need to promise yourself now that you will do these challenges to the best of your ability. Some will seem silly but worthwhile. Others will be more practical to your daily life. All of them are meant to help you push forward into a more creative and productive space.

Pre-Game Challenge

Because today is only an introduction, we'll keep this one simple, but it will still test many of you.

First, stand in a quiet room, upright, proud and tall. Stand with your head up, chest out, arms back. Now stare into the open space of the room and imagine there is a figure standing in front of you. This figure is FEAR. Imagine what this feeling looks like to you in a physical form. Humanize FEAR so that you have a figure you can address for a short conversation. Imagine that FEAR is snarling at you, trying to intimidate you into backing down. Imagine how scary FEAR looks from across the room. Feel the FEAR—embrace it.

Now, extend one arm, with your hand open, palm facing you. While staring directly at FEAR, without wavering, close your forefinger into your palm, and then your ring finger. Follow that with your thumb, and your pinky.

Stand defiantly in the face of FEAR with your middle finger extended proudly. Shout or say loudly, "F**k FEAR, Screw FEAR, or Forget FEAR." This sounds profane, but do it. I promise, this will be liberating.

As you stand there with your hand proudly extended in the face of FEAR, imagine the monster getting so upset that it charges at you. Imagine what it would feel like to be attacked. Imagine how fast it would cross the room to you. Picture the snarling beast as it lunges at you while you stand strong.

What happened? Nothing, right? You weren't hurt or killed. You didn't crumple to the floor. You stood up to FEAR, and you came out without a scratch. You're unscathed, because of course, it was imaginary.

Finally, do your best Rocky imitation. Throw your hands up into the air in a victory pose, and do so with authority. Give a hooting shout to your achievement, if you feel the urge, or jump up and down. Be proud of yourself. You just tackled your first level of FEAR. There will be more, but relish in this victory now.

Congratulations! This is how the process works. This is how it feels to win.

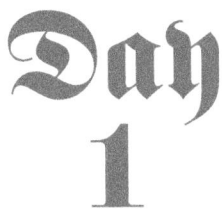

Day
1

FEED THE MACHINE

Let's talk about the starving artist mentality for a moment, because I know there are plenty of you who fall into this category, whether you believe it or not. Allow me to illustrate a problem for you with the help of some bread and luncheon meat.

I'm sure you can relate to this scenario: You see an attractive, yet wafer-thin girl walking down the street in tight pants or a short skirt. Her body is slight; as if a heavy gust of wind would send her off to Oz in a moment. Your initial reaction is, "Damn, girl, eat a sandwich."

Now, of course, it's wrong, malicious, and downright hateful to make that judgement, but we all do it. We judge the girl based on her appearance, without knowing her story. Maybe her tiny frame comes from genetics and a healthy metabolism. Maybe she's suffering from a debilitating eating disorder that she tries to hide from public eyes, even if we can see the symptoms in her profile. We don't know this woman, but it doesn't stop us from spitting hurtful comments under our breath—why? Because we're haters, and it makes us feel better to knock on others so that we don't have to deal with our own situation for that brief moment.

Maybe that girl really is hungry. Perhaps she does have an eating disorder, and really needs a kind person to lend her support. She might have family and *friends* who tell her she's fat, despite the projected collarbones. Perhaps what she really needs is a good friend to let her know she deserves better.

The *starving artist* is the same.

The starving artist's problem is also a disorder, a manifestation of ideas drilled into them over many years. They get told they can't make a life as an artist, or that it's a badge of honor to kill themselves for your art, with no chance of reward until they've put in decades of work first. Then, if they're lucky, there might be a chance someone will pay attention.

They are told by their peers that they should sooner give their art away than sell it, because art is about expression and shouldn't be about a paycheck. The starving artist fears becoming a sellout, even if the interpretation of the term has been tainted. These creative souls can't help their misguided beliefs. It's what they've been told since they were young—that an artist must struggle and feel pain to be a true success, and money should be an afterthought.

In all my years working with creative people, one thing always rings true: A majority of the creative battle is fought within our thoughts and actions, not in our techniques, skills, or tactics. Developing a new outlook on our lives can bring as much success, if not more, to our business. Marketing techniques come and go, but a positive mindset is forever...and contagious.

In this journey, I try to be that good friend who tells you what you *need* to hear instead of what you *want* to hear. I'm also here to reassure you that you deserve better.

There are many paths to take from this moment unto success, and the lessons that follow can help you navigate that pilgrimage, regardless of the exact path you are on. I have no doubt that if you implement these ideas into your game plan, you will do more with your work than you ever have in the past.

Every single creative individual, whether struggling or successful, has moments of desperation. They read books, listen to podcasts, and take classes to find new ways to elevate their business. However, the real answers are not in tactics, but in deep mindset methods.

I take these lessons to be essential elements that run consistent with every successful entrepreneur I have met. Does each entrepreneur possess them completely? No, but they do implement these methods as thoroughly as possible in an effort to guarantee success.

Even though we're on a path of daily ritual, there is a lot to implement. Do not try to overhaul your psyche in one sitting. That will not work, and you will burn out. Instead, apply these methods a little at a time. Hone those few to excellence, and then apply others. You won't nail them all, and you will occasionally fail, but with diligence and perseverance successes will start showing a change in the way you look and feel about your business.

Challenge 1

Find five people in your list of family and friends who haven't been the most supportive of you in the past. Share with them that you are trying to take your business to a new level, and you would appreciate if they would share your shop link or website with their family and friends. You can even create a bit of *swipe copy* for them to use, or let them word it their own way.

When you reach out, make sure the note is direct but personable. Write a new note for each individual so you do not come off as canned. Let them know that you would appreciate their support, and then wait for their responses. If they share it, thank them.

If they do not want to share, ask them why. You don't want to make them feel guilty, but ask what you can do to make them feel comfortable with sharing the work. There might be a lesson for you in your approach.

If they don't respond at all, move on. Do not dwell on those who don't support you. Instead, go hang out with the ones who have your back, and return the favor if you can.

Now that you've done that, do it again. Find five more people and repeat the process. If you don't have five more, then maybe you need to expand your network. We'll get into that more in another challenge.

Finally, give yourself a high-five for tackling another FEAR monster. Stamp another *kill* mark on the side of your fuselage. This could get to be a habit.

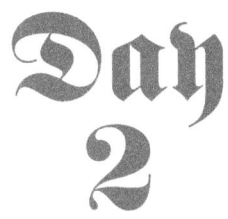

Day 2

WE DO WHAT WE DO

...because we cannot do anything else.

You may very well be the most talented person in your circle of influence, but does that mean you're doing what you truly should be doing with your life? Do you even know what it means to do the kind of work that fulfills you inside and out? Can you define your true purpose—the one thing that you could be content doing the rest of your life that also provides value to the world at the same time?

If you don't know the answer to that question, don't sweat it just yet. It's a huge question, and many people don't know where to begin to use their skills, talent, and knowledge to make a positive impact on the world. It took me over forty years before I realized I was put here on the planet to help artists, designers, and other creatives become better at what they do. In all fairness, had I been more focused and attentive earlier on in life, I might have been here sooner. But no regrets, I'm here now, and I'm attacking that purpose with ferocity.

The question remains, how do you find that purpose if you don't know where to start? The truth is there is no single answer to the question. I found mine after spending countless years drifting through projects that sounded like the right idea at the time, but didn't give me the fulfillment I needed. I worked on various art and design projects because they were an expression of my artistic skill, but it wasn't the creative act that made me feel good.

Instead, it was the conversations I had with other creative people about their work that empowered me. I enjoyed talking to them about their projects, lending my insight about design, marketing and media to help them improve. In retrospect, I can look back on my life and realize I was always doing this, for free, and loving it.

How you find your purpose could be vastly different, but it starts with being 100% honest with yourself on the topic. Start by asking yourself some questions.

- When you were a child, what did you want to be when you grew up?
- How does that match up to your wants and desires today?
- What were you doing the last time you felt pure joy in your work?
- If money was no concern, what kind of work would you do?

Granted, when you were a child, you may have wanted to be a fireman or a doctor, but that might not be your purposeful direction now. These questions aren't meant to define your purpose so much as they are meant to help you think about what makes you happy. Once you remember what it's like to be happy with work in mind, then you may better recognize what makes you happy about the work you currently do. There's also the chance it lets you know what work you absolutely do *not* like. Even if you can't find your true purpose right off, at the very least, you will know what you don't want to do. As you move through all the things you don't want to do, by process of elimination, you get closer to what satisfies your needs.

One thing to note is that your purpose doesn't have to be some altruistic endeavor. It doesn't need to be charitable or require you to go on a spiritual crusade. It can be as simple as understanding what work you should be selling to which types of people, and being perfectly OK with that as your path. The beauty of this is that you get to define your purpose—nobody else gets to tell you what your purpose should be. All the world cares about is that you find that purpose and get to work on it as soon as possible. There are problems to be solved, needs to be filled, and the sooner you get to it the better.

Challenge 2

Take a notebook and a pen and write down all the things you love about the work you do. Focus on what brings you the most joy. Then write down all the things that you don't care for in your work, the things you would eliminate if you could.

If the second list is bigger than the first, you might have a problem with your purpose. If that's the case, maybe it's time to ask yourself the questions above and see if you can tap into what satisfies you more than anything.

Again, honesty is the best tool you have in this process. If you're not totally honest in answering these questions, you're only hurting yourself. The answers you find may end up taking you down an entirely different path, away from your creative goals, but if it's where your heart belongs, then maybe it's time for a change.

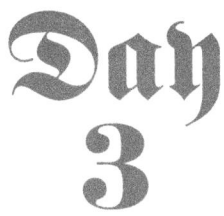

Day 3

LISTEN TO YOUR MOMMA

When I was young, my mom always encouraged my creative behavior. She told me I could become an artist or illustrator, or that I should focus on my writing. When I was a young adult, she said I should get into voice acting, because I had a unique voice and an interesting way of expressing myself.

Of course I did what any young adult would do when their mother offers unsolicited life lessons…I ignored her. Jump ahead a couple decades and I have created a world where I make money from my art, my writing, and my voice. My mother never had to say, "I told you so," because I think it for her on a regular basis.

Even after yesterday's challenge, some of you may be lost for a clear direction in your work. If you're trying to find your way in this world and you're not quite sure which path to follow, think back to the things your mother or father constantly told you about what they believed were your gifts. Your purpose might exist somewhere in those sentiments, and they saw it in you long ago.

That said, it doesn't have to be parents, because I know some of you might have a contentious relationship with the parental units. Instead, maybe it's an older sibling, a trusting aunt, or a longtime friend. It could be a teacher or a mentor you had as a kid, or it could even be that gut instinct that still burns inside you about the things you never pursued but always wanted. Someone, somewhere knew from the beginning what you had within, but you were too preoccupied with other interests to pay attention. If you know who this trusted soul is, maybe now is a good time to reach out to them.

Have a conversation with them, ask them questions about your past, and perhaps within those shared words is the answer to your quandary. Your purpose may exist in the eyes of others and what they saw in you. There's only one way to find out.

Challenge 3

It's time for a phone call. Pick up the phone and call your mom, dad, or whoever it is that you feel knows the answer to the following question:

"What direction did you expect me to head when I was young?"

You should expand on that question and dig deeper. Make sure they know they can be totally honest with you. In turn, you should be ready to hear what they tell you.

What they share may not resonate with you at all anymore, and that's fine. These conversations are not about finding a direct path to the answer, but rather, opening your mind to new ideas you may not have considered before. The conversation may not give you the *aha* moment you want, but it may lead you down a path that gives the answer you need.

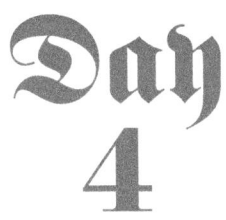

Day 4

99 PROBLEMS, BUT A NICHE AIN'T ONE

Whom do you serve? Can you picture them in your mind? Can you call them out by name? I'm not talking about the friends and family who buy your stuff because they feel like they should support your *little hobby*. I mean the anonymous people who come to your online shop and buy your products without knowing anything about you. How well do you know them?

You may not know the intimate details about your customers, but that doesn't mean you can't define them. There are certain aspects about the people who buy your products that you may know but take for granted.

Recently, I had a conversation with a client who creates both art and jewelry around a common theme. She realized that many of her clients were buying her products as wedding presents, or gifts from the bride to her wedding party. Nobody had to beat her over the head twice to make her realize who she should be promoting her work toward. She has recently refocused her branding and marketing efforts to cater to this wedding crowd, and it seems to be paying off, certainly in sales, but also in the satisfaction of knowing she found a market for business that fits her intent. She can still sell her art and crafts to people not looking for wedding gifts, of course, but the clearer focus on a particular market has made her approach to her business more fluid.

One important aspect about her picking this niche is that she knows brides do not scrimp on expenses for their wedding, if they can avoid it. They are inclined to spend money where it counts. My client understands that knowing her niche is only part of the issue. She also understands that the customers in that niche are willing to pay the kind of money needed to afford her work. This is an essential part of the equation. You may know who your potential customers are, but if they can't afford you, or are not inclined to pay your prices, then they really don't have as much potential as you expect.

If you can identify what kind of person your ideal customer is, then you have a better chance of identify their passions. We want passions over interests because we want customers who are passionate instead of just interested. When you can tap into the subjects that people get stark raving mad over (animal lovers, paleo fiends, cosplay fanatics, brides), that's where you find the wellspring of buyers. That is where the money flows.

Challenge 4

We're going to try to identify what kind of people buy your work, or if it's a gift, who the gift is for. On a piece of paper, identify your ideal customer, best as possible, by writing down all the attributes that make sense to someone who would buy your work the moment they saw it. You may want to go as far as creating a fictitious customer right down to their personal attributes, family life, and what kind of work they do. The FBI would call this suspect profiling, but we'll call it buyer creation.

Second, brainstorm all the different niches this ideal customer might be a part of in relation to your work. What are their passions, and how can you use that to your advantage in creating a niche for yourself? If you sell hand-dyed fabric and textiles, and your ideal customer is a midwestern empty-nester who likes quilting, then how can you serve that niche in a way that taps into their needs, but still leaves you available to customers outside that niche?

The identity of your ideal customer will likely change over time, but every time you go through this exercise to identify them, the easier it gets—and you more accurately identify who you should spend your time marketing toward.

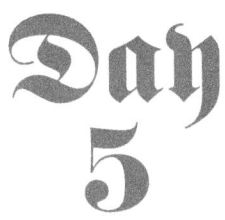

Day 5

CHASE YOUR DREAM, NOT SOMEONE ELSE'S

You have your dream, and that dream is awesome. Your creative pursuit is important and you should follow it. However, the viability of that pursuit as a business may or may not be strong. There is a chance you will get rich from it, but avoid the temptation to chase someone else's dream just because you see them doing well.

I'm sure you've seen the Keep Calm and Carry On posters, or any of their derivatives. They are ubiquitous around the Internet because so many people have copied that design in an effort to ride the coattails of success, and gain sales. Anytime there is a new, popular meme, the same ritual gets played out everywhere. Go to Etsy right now and search for any current pop culture reference and see how many people are trying to capitalize on its popularity. A search for Breaking Bad nets a return of more than 6,000 images at the time of this writing. Game of Thrones brings 22,000. I don't even need to get into the impropriety of trademark infringement.

This copycat method never works for the long term, unless you're a manufacturing plant in China. Constantly chasing someone else's success will never bring you the fulfillment you're seeking. It may fill the pockets of the copycats for awhile, but when that meme loses traction, these creatively challenged makers must find a new trend to glom onto.

The ironic thing about copying someone else's dream is that you can follow someone else's lead, produce their kind of work, follow their method to the letter, and you still will not see the same results they produced. Too many factors are at play beyond the scope of the work, how it was implemented, and how they market it. Their success is built not only on their business efforts, but their life experience. You cannot copy that, so stop trying to make it happen.

Go find your dream—the thing that burns inside you and will not be snuffed out. Chase that until success or failure. If you maintain your authenticity, do the work, and stay the course, you will succeed.

Challenge 5

Sit down and take a good look at your portfolio of work. If there is anything in there that does not resonate with you, or you only did it to cater to an external need or trend, consider removing it from your offerings. If it's a popular item, ride it out while you can (as long as it's legal). While you wait for that trend to pass, work on making your products and services the most authentic you can to your mission and purpose.

Brutal honesty is at play here. If you are not honest with yourself, this only leads to a less fulfilling business experience. Do what's inside you. Become the trend others follow.

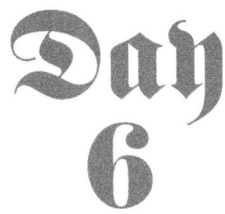

DON'T BE VANILLA

In horse racing, any horse that does not qualify in 1st, 2nd, or 3rd place is referred to as an *also-ran*. If could decide your place in the race of life, why would you ever choose to be an *also-ran*?

In business, there are plenty of people working to be *also-rans* in their niche. I have never understood why anyone would go into a market filled with competitors, all working with similar products or methods, with the intention to do the exact same thing as everyone else. It baffles me.

For example, let's look at a few recent, popular trends. How many cupcake shops or food trucks opened up in the past few years because they saw other people doing well with them? How many retro barber shops? What if instead of becoming the next cupcake purveyor, you made the best handmade scones anyone has ever tasted? While new people open up food trucks every day, the successful food truck owners are going back and opening restaurants, because it's much harder to create a unique dining experience when your kitchen is on four wheels.

Food trucks are a less expensive means to an end, but how many trucks have tried and failed because they only wanted to win the next Great Food Truck Race? (Is that even still a thing?) The funny thing about most food trucks, while everyone else was trying to figure out the best way to put things into taco shells, my favorite truck was doing something revolutionary…making hot dogs.

Dogzilla is a popular truck here in Southern California with a unique take on hot dogs. They put whole-beef dogs into King's Hawaiian buns and top them with all sorts of unique Asian-inspired toppings. It sounds crazy, but their dogs are the BOMB, and they sell like crazy because they're not your typical food truck fare. They separate themselves in a crowded market by going outside the norm.

If you are determined to jump into a saturated market, instead of keeping up with the Joneses, you better *be* the Joneses. Frosted Cupcakery is a local bakery that came into the market partway into the cupcake surge. At a disadvantage because of timing, they came in with something to prove. Their cupcakes are by far the best I have tasted, and I've tried plenty. I'm a cupcake fiend, and every time I see a new shop, I have to do my comparison shopping. Really, though, there is no comparison—Frosted kills them all with a quality product that is second to none. The lines out the door, even after several years in business, prove they do business the right way.

The lesson here is, of course, to be as original as you can. If you can't get to true originality, be the best at whatever it is you do.

Find a way to set yourself apart in the crowds. In other words, stop trying to be everyone's favorite vanilla. Instead, be different—be mint chocolate chip. In fact, don't stop at different, but strive to be something people either love or hate. In the fight for attention, it's always better to polarize people's opinions than to be run-of-the-mill.

Challenge 6

If you still have your notebook open from yesterday's challenge, take note of your products or services, and try to find areas where you can expand or diversify your line in unique and interesting ways, while still maintaining your core values.

What can you offer that is endemically you, but still allows you to separate yourself from the competition? If you sell bath and body products, what's different about your bath bombs? If you teach art classes, how do you interject your personality and style into the work so you don't come off like any other art instructor?

The differences might be subtle, or they could be a complete departure from form. The latter might be a painful reality, but by doing so, you open yourself up to new opportunities because you took a chance on separating yourself from the crowd.

Finally, go treat yourself to some ice cream. You deserve it for making it this far already.

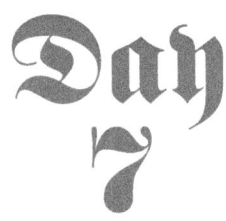

Day 7

TAKE CHANCES, MAKE MISTAKES, & GET MESSY

One of my son's favorite cartoons is the Magic School Bus. This show is a little after my time, but I don't mind him watching it, because there's a lot of educational value within the lessons. My favorite lesson comes from the main character, Miss Frizzle, where she announces each episode that they should, "take chances, make mistakes, and get messy," which is so counterintuitive to our normal process. As adults, we forget what it was like to let go and not worry about getting paint on the walls. As kids, we only cared about having fun, and worried about getting scolded by our parents after.

Whatever work you do, I'm sure you're good at it, or you're at least getting better all the time. You have your process down pat and you're a production machine. Maybe you're selling a lot, but you're losing the passion for the work. I've seen that happen up close; people get so caught up in their business they forget the creativity that got them there.

The best way I know to invigorate your work is to experiment with it—take chances. Whether you're a painter, sculptor, photographer, or writer, take time to play with the work. Push the boundaries of what you normally do and make something totally outside the norm. It might suck, and it may not work, but at least you tried something new. And you may end up discovering more about yourself.

At one point in my career, I made the mistake of putting my art aside for the sake of a job, and it was the worst thing I could for my creative mind. Don't put aside the creativity for the sake of the dollar bills. Instead, find a way to play and experiment while you're working on other things. The only way you grow is by trying new things and getting outside our normal boundaries.

The only way to succeed in your creative work is to constantly grow. Your customers may not say they want you to push your limits, but silently, it's what they expect.

Challenge 7

Set aside a decent amount of time to work on a new project. Instead of thinking of this as something you can sell, consider it a personal project with no expectations of anything beyond the process. This is R&D time.

Don't worry about the amount of time it takes. Don't think about what it will look like when you're done. Just sit down, work, and have fun. Acknowledge your efforts while you're working without making any judgement. That will be difficult, but perhaps you can learn something about your process.

There are no rules and no mistakes. If you flub something, let it happen and figure out how to incorporate it into the work. Be completely unencumbered and see what happens. Enjoy the time spent, and appreciate it whether the work is good or not. You're not in this to be self-critical.

For now, play. The business stuff can always come later.

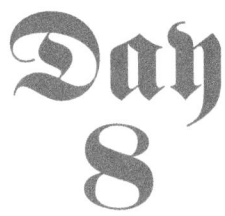

Day 8

RESPECT THE PROCESS

The best thing about being an artist and designer is that I get to spend long periods of time working on projects centered around my own creativity. Sure, a significant portion of that time is spent in production mode, knitting the creative impulses together, but those webs of busywork are just as essential to the process. In the past, when working on a lengthy project, I would get impatient because I was focused on the final result. I wanted the work to be done quicker so I could do something with the piece. I wanted it done so I could send it off to a customer and get started on the next one, but this removed a lot of the joy from the work.

Recently, I had a fan of my podcast ask a question regarding a similar problem she was having. She spent so much time working on the business end of her art she almost forgot how to look at a blank canvas without anticipating the finished work. She looked at every piece of art as something to be sold instead of the creativity it beheld. If the starving artist is the one who dares not consider the commercial aspects of their work, then this would be the antithesis—the *voracious entrepreneur*, perhaps.

I've never been one to meditate, at least in the most traditional sense of sitting in silence in an effort to ground myself in the moment. However, at times while I'm working, I find myself getting into a zone of creative consciousness. I'm hustling along at smooth but rapid pace, and the work is almost effortless. When I discovered this about myself, I realized that I was in a near-meditative state and felt very connected to the work. I knew I was on a path with the piece because every brush stroke or mouse click felt predestined. Perhaps coincidentally, the work that came from those sessions turned out to be some of my best. I was less concerned about the final product and more involved in the process of making.

It is my belief that if we spent less time concerned about what our work will do when it leaves our hands, and are more thoughtful of the effort to make it, we will become more fulfilled and satisfied. When you are more satisfied with the work you're doing, you can't help but express yourself in a way that intrigues others. You share the work because you're so happy with the way it made you feel, and when you're a happy creative, your customers want some of that. Embrace the process of creating, and it will lead you to a more satisfying business environment.

Challenge 8

The next project you work on, take some time to really appreciate the efforts. Consider every movement you make and acknowledge how it took you from one moment into the next. Think about how your micro-actions move the project along.

If you're a painter, really feel the brush strokes, and watch the paint as it interacts with the substrate.

If you're a photographer, consider the changes in light and the adjustment of the settings. Think about the composition and how other parts of the shot are interacting with your main subject.

If you're a writer, forget about editing, and just let the words fly onto the page. Dwell on how your fingers touch the keys, or hand pushes the pen across the paper.

Whatever it is you do, examine the tiny details of how you do your work, and consider each action as a step toward something awesome. Be OK with mistakes, and let the work be nothing more than a way for you to express yourself. Appreciate the rituals for what they will become if you allow yourself to do what comes natural.

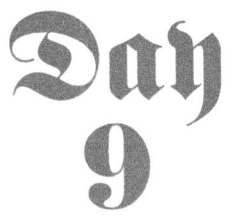

Day 9

START A LIST!

I put an exclamation point up there for a reason—to get you to pay attention. If you do any one thing for your business that you haven't done yet, let this be the one.

If you have an active and engaged email list now, you can skip today. I promise we have more tasty challenges coming your way. If you have not started an email list yet, allow me to express how crazy-foolish that is.

There once was a crafty lass who loved the Internet so much, she put all of her work online. Unfortunately, she never saw the benefit of investing in her platform, and she only used free services to build her business. She sold her work on Etsy and promoted her products through social media, and things were going great. Then one day, an evil queen saw the lass and was jealous of her success, so she used her minions to unleash a storm of spam reports and faulty accusations of copyright infringement. Practically overnight, the young woman saw all her hard work turn to ash because her social media accounts were blocked and her Etsy shop was closed by the administration. Now she had no way to get in touch with her customers and fans, and her business was doomed. If only she had some way to communicate to her customer base about the unfortunate changes while she regrouped and built her business up again. Unfortunately, she built her foundation on soft ground, and now she must start again from scratch.

That's a bit of a dramatic tale, but not so far removed from reality. When you rely on other services to maintain your customer and fan lists, you put yourself at risk if anything changes within those spaces. If the woman in the above story had an email list established, she could easily send out updates to her people about the changes and when they could expect her to be back up and selling again. Instead of allowing Etsy to control her customer interaction, she could have taken charge of it herself. The beauty of having a list is that no matter what happens to your accounts, you get to keep your contacts for life.

Throughout this challenge, I will talk about the most important things I've done for my business, and building a list is definitely in the top three. I would be nothing without my list, so I cherish, grow, and protect it the best I can. Those people saw fit to give me their precious email address, and I would never consider abusing that trust. My list is a valuable tool, and I make sure to provide high-quality content to them on a regular basis. By doing so, I am rewarded with good interaction, referrals, and sales.

Now some of you may be thinking, "But I don't know what to write about." That, my friends, is a cop-out, and I will not let you get away with it. If you searched *what to write in my newsletter* into Google, you would get back a deluge of responses, and almost all of them could be catered to your readership in some way or another. There are no excuses to making this happen, especially since MailChimp will allow anyone to have an email list service for free (with some limitations).

In the future, email may not be the best way to communicate with your customers and fans, but until someone invents the next killer app to knock email off its throne, you should make list building a top priority in your business.

Challenge 9

Go to MailChimp.com and sign up for a free account. Once you have that open, write your first message that goes out to everyone who signs up. It can be as simple as giving thanks for allowing you into their inbox. If you want to be extra generous, give them something for free. You don't have to create a month-long challenge like this, but I'm sure you can come up with something cool.

Next, create a form with MailChimp's form builder and then find a place to post that form so people can sign up to your list. Make sure to keep it above the fold (first part of your site that people see when they visit, without having to scroll down), and don't be meek about it. Make it visible enough for people to want to join.

Now pat yourself on the back for being awesome and smart.

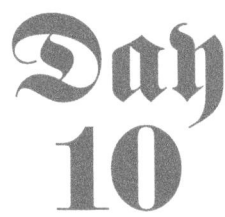

Day 10

PLAY TO YOUR STRENGTHS—DELEGATE YOUR WEAKNESSES

Let's face it, there is some stuff you're just not good at in your business. For me, it's accounting and staying focused on tasks. Maybe for you it's graphic design, writing copy, or managing your inventory. Whatever it is, there are things you're *getting by* on in your business because you don't feel you have the need or resources to hire someone to do them for you. However, that mindset does you and your business a disservice.

When you try to be all things to your business, you cripple yourself with the ideology that you must run your shop all by yourself to remain pure and authentic to your craft. It's not an uncommon thought, one suffered by almost every business person at some point. You might believe you can't afford to hire someone to help you in those trouble areas, but allow me to illustrate that you can't afford to <u>not</u> hire someone to do the heavy lifting in areas where you are weakest.

Imagine, if you will, in your business, you pay yourself a rate of $50 an hour. That's $50 an hour for all the creative work (fair), the bookkeeping (maybe), the social media updates (too much), stocking the shelves, and taking out the garbage (H-E-double-hockey-sticks NO). Would you pay someone to come to your office to tidy up for $50 an hour? Of course not, but you do every day because you're acting as the tidy-upper, and we already agreed what you're paying yourself.

Now imagine you hired someone to come in and do your social media and stock your shelves and fulfill order for $25 an hour. Not only are you paying less overall, but they might be able to do it faster than you since they aren't splitting their time between other things. And now you can focus your $50 energy on projects that warrant that cost, like new ideas and creativity.

This may sound like a bit of a stretch, but one way I delegate a responsibility is by having a gardener do my yard work. I have massive hay fever allergies, and I hate doing yard work in general, so the first thing I got help doing was the gardening. Since I work from home, and I also have a rental property in the back of my house, I can hire a gardener as a tax write-off. He can be picking weeds and trimming hedges while I spend time working on my next project.

Maybe you're not making enough money yet to hire an employee, but consider for a moment that there are small things in your business that you might be able to delegate—to pay a freelancer for instead of doing it yourself. I'm sure just by bringing up this topic there is at least one task that you wish you could eliminate from your personal to-do list. Maybe you don't have my same gardener situation, but I'm sure there is something you could benefit from handing certain tasks to someone else.

From now on, every time you start working on something new in your business, take a moment to ask yourself, "Is this a $50 job or not?" If the answer is no, then it's time to add that to the list of things you should probably be outsourcing. Talk to any successful business owner and they will tell you that one of the best decisions they made for their business was outsourcing an aspect of the work to someone who could do it better, faster, and cheaper.

Challenge 10

Pick at least one part of your business that you do not like to do on your own, whether that's marketing, accounting, production work, or cleaning up the office. Next, brainstorm ways to give the task to someone else. Consider how much time it takes you to do that work now, and how much money you could save if you put that job in someone else's hands while you do the work that makes you happy, or that you especially excel at.

There are certain things you should never give to others, though. The creative work should always be yours. Also, if there is a story to be told in your promotional efforts, make sure it's you telling the story and not some hired hand. You want to maintain your voice in the business, always.

Aside from that caveat, go nuts. If you're feeling frisky, make a list of things you would like to eliminate from your task list. Email me and tell me what work you'd like to give to someone else so you can get back to the cool stuff: dave@freshrag.com.

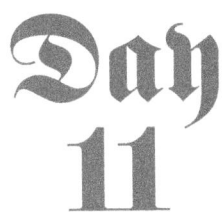

Day 11

SALVATION THROUGH AUTOMATION

Can I tell you a secret?

In the past, I was a chronic flake when it came to my schedule. Left to my own devices, and a lack of a calendar, I would forget any and all birthdays, anniversaries, and appointments. If there was an Olympic sport for missing important dates, I would win the gold medal every time. I'm convinced it's a disease of an overstimulated mind—blame it on my adult A.D.D.

When I finally got smart about how bad I am at keeping my schedule, I implemented software to help me keep track of things. I use a service called Schedule Once to help me schedule meetings and events, and now instead of me having to check my calendar for timing conflicts for meet-ups with others, I can give someone a simple URL to follow and they can schedule something that fits in my open time slots. Then all I need to do is check my calendar each morning, which is something I've programmed myself to do, finally.

That example is automation at its simplest form, and it's helped me change how I do work. Another example of automation that helps me get things done is this email series. I'm sure it's no surprise that these messages are coming to you over a timed sequence depending on when you signed up. Each message is programmed by smarter people than me to be delivered to your email inbox at a prescribed time after the previous message. If I had to remember to send these notes out each day to you all, I would most certainly forget and screw it up (see example above). Instead, I employ software to help me out.

I also use automation to get my messages out to the public. Whether that's Hootsuite, Buffer, or MeetEdgar, I have scheduled messages that go out to my Facebook and Twitter feeds on a random schedule. Instead of me spending countless hours on social media, I can be working on other things while the messages go out. I always come back to check and see if I can interact with people who have responded to my scheduled messages, but my time spent on those platforms is radically diminished, and I am far more productive.

As technology grows, we are finding more and more ways to automate our lives. Some are good, and others not so much, but if we use the services to our benefit (and the benefit of our fans and customers), then we can create a workflow that helps boost our business while still maintaining a connection to the world.

Is there a part of your daily rituals that you spend way too much time working on but wish you could get off your plate? Maybe automation is the key.

Challenge 11

Think about all the things you do that you call *work* but are really nothing but time being sucked out of your day. Can you apply some automation so you do not have to be so hands-on?

Maybe it's automated emails that go out to customers after an order, or a set of tweets that get scheduled to share at certain times. Locate the *time suck* moments, and find a way to put software to work for you.

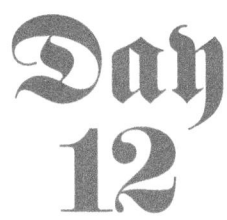

Day 12

FIND REGIMEN

As I mentioned earlier, automating my calendar is essential to my success. However, there's more to managing a schedule than having a convenient link to give people so they can add themselves into my schedule. If I didn't have a finely tuned schedule, I would have people booking time slots at all hours of the day, interrupting my flow. This is not how productivity happens.

Instead, I make sure to micromanage my calendar almost to a point of absurdity. My calendar has time slots for all aspects of my life, both work and personal, and this helps me stay on task. Between 6 and 8am, it's parental duties. 8 to 10am is time for me to work out, eat breakfast, and clean up. 10am to 1pm is usually my time for meetings and podcast interviews. 1 to 5pm is when I do my writing and creative work. At 5pm, my schedule stops because that's when I pick up the boy from day care, and it's back to being Daddy time.

I put this time blocking in place to create ritual with my day. The repetition allows me to create habits, and those habits create a highly productive work situation. Am I perfect at maintaining the regimen? No, but I try hard to maintain the schedule so I can keep both my work and my life in a state of flow.

This is my schedule, and it works for me, but yours might be different. It's important for you to know when is the best time for you to do your thing. Do you create better in the morning or in the evening? Are there large blocks of time when you can schedule certain activities, or do you have smaller blocks that require tasks to be broken up?

Using your bigger deadlines as gauges, take some time to figure out how to best break up your day into segments that allow you to gain control of your schedule. Set times for work, and times for play as well. It's important to set aside time for yourself, to chill, or to be with family.

Once you have a schedule, make agreements with yourself, your partners, and your family that you will be doing X during these hours, and Y during other hours. Then go do X and Y during those times. You don't have to finish, and you don't have to beat yourself up during that time to feel like you accomplished something. Spend the time, do the work, and then stop.

It's also a good idea to not cross timelines, especially when tapping into family time. The more compromises you make with your schedule, the quicker it can go off the rails. If you've decided to work on a project until 5pm—stop at 5pm. Of course, day-to-day operations will conflict, especially if you have kids, and if you falter one day or another, don't try to make it up the next. Stick to the schedule, put in honest work, and you will finish what you started on time.

Regimen takes diligence and practice. It will not come overnight, and you will make adjustments constantly to fit in changes in your daily life. Schedule as much of your life as you can, though, and it will help you become more productive.

Challenge 12

If you find that your schedule is chaotic, sit down with your favorite daily calendar and consider what times of day are best for the different parts of your life. Start blocking your time off and practice it for a week. Adjust what doesn't work, add in things you forgot to dedicate time toward, and note tasks that should be outsourced, automated, or eliminated completely.

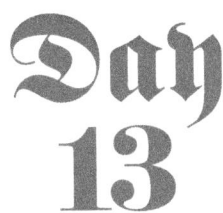

Day 13

F.O.C.U.S.

That acronym stands for Follow One Course Until Success, and I believe it's something every creative person should use as a personal mantra, because I know how easy it is to get distracted by new things.

As creatives, we have a tendency to do what I refer to as chasing butterflies, jumping from one idea to another as each comes into view. Ideas to artists are like a laser pointer to a cat; one flick and that kitty is off chasing the red dot wherever it goes—off a ledge, perhaps.

I propose that instead of chasing every single idea down, trying to implement it right away, we find one or two ideas that complement each other and benefit the core work we do, and then focus on them until you achieve success.

My site, FreshRag.com has had a storied life in its relatively short existence. The site started as a curated art blog, became a blog about paper arts, and then fell into a pit of despair with no content going out. Finally, when I realized the potential of the content was creative, and what my true purpose was, I stopped chasing random ideas that crossed my path. I turned Fresh Rag into the resource it is today—helping creatives grow their business. Only after I found my purpose and focused on it did I start seeing real growth.

New ideas are good. You should always strive for new ideas, but just because you have an idea does not mean you have to act on it. Hold onto all your ideas, but don't feel compelled to follow them all immediately. Instead, get a notebook just for writing down all your fancy new ideas. Anytime an idea strikes you, write it in the notebook, one idea per page. That way you can go back and add notes to the different ideas as new concepts come to you.

The problem with ideas is that we may not know which ones we should chase, and which to hold over. In his book, the $100 Startup, Chris Guillebeau advises us to ask ourselves three questions before jumping into any new idea.

1. How will I get paid with this idea?
2. How much would I get paid from this idea?
3. Is there a way I could get paid more than once?

If one idea starts to resonate more with you than others—and you aren't focusing your energy elsewhere—go for it! If an idea sounds good but doesn't fit within the work you're trying to accomplish at the moment, go ahead and mine that coal, but stash it away, and bring it out when you need a diamond.

Until then, F.O.C.U.S. on the goal at hand, and let the other butterflies fly free.

Challenge 13

Time for some hard, self-truth time. Think about all the projects you're working on right now, or the ones you're contemplating. How many of them work toward the core of what you're trying to accomplish with your business? If many of them do fit into your plan, which ones can you focus on right now for the best success, and which ones can you put off?

Get a notebook and start writing down all the other *someday* ideas. Revisit that list on a regular basis. If the day comes when it feels like the right time to implement a particular idea, move it to the top of your priorities. If not, maybe it's time to let that idea go.

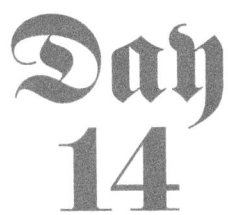

BE FEARLESS!

Let's talk about your brain for a moment. There's this part of your mind commonly referred to as your *lizard brain*. It's the part of your psyche responsible for keeping you out of harm's way. Sometimes it's important to listen to the lizard brain (e.g., don't walk down dark alleys at night, be careful of hot surfaces, look both ways before crossing the street), but often the lizard just wants to keep you inside the comfort zone, to not step out into unfamiliar territory. The lizard brain is not an entrepreneur.

If you ask me, they should call it something different. Lizard brain is too cute—something to not worry about. Who's afraid of small animals that lick their own eyeballs? Instead, I believe it should be named demon head, ogre brain, or phantom mind. Do you think you'd pay attention to a phantom when it's trying to *protect* you? I'm more inclined to call an exorcist.

Phantom mind attacks your will, your drive, and your passion. It keeps you from achieving anything awesome because it wants to keep you all to itself. Most of the time, we are compelled to succumb to the phantom, but I say, fight the phantom. Be fearless. Charge into your dreams without fear.

Remember what we said about fear at the start of this journey? It's mostly a myth. That thing you are afraid of, the one that holds you back—just like monsters in the closet—doesn't exist. The moment you step into that fear and come out the other side, you realize it wasn't worth being scared of. When you find yourself backing away from something out of fear or instinct, ask yourself, "What is the absolute worst thing that could happen?" I don't care what it is you're thinking of doing or creating, there is a strong probability you won't die or go to jail over it, so why be scared?

Unless you're a soldier fighting in the Middle East, a deep-sea welder, or an Alaskan crab fisherman, you have little to worry about in your daily life. Your fears are largely comprised of new social norms. Back when we were not the apex predator on the planet, our lizard brain kept us safe from things like volcanoes and saber-toothed cats. Since those times, our lizard brain has made adjustments to what it believes we need protection from. What was once a saber-toothed cat is now diminished to "What are people saying about me on Twitter?" These fears are unfounded—squash them! Charge into your dreams as if you can't lose. Even if you fail, at least you will learn from the experience, and you can try again. Be fearless, and don't let the *phantom mind* control how brave you are.

Challenge 14

Think of one thing you've been telling yourself you need to do but you've put off because it was unfamiliar territory. Now, find a way to make it happen, whatever it takes. Simple, but not easy. Commit to it until you succeed, and I promise the next time you step into unfamiliar territory, it will be easier.

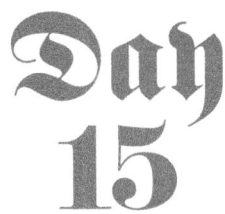

FIND A MENTOR

When I flew the coop on my day job, I felt overwhelmed by all the things I didn't know about being a solo entrepreneur. I craved knowledge and understanding, but I knew what I needed wouldn't be found in a business book. Instead, I sought out the help of a business professional to help guide me on my new journey. In retrospect, I am certain that my self-awareness, knowing I needed help, and then going to get the help, made a huge difference in how much my business progressed in the first few years. It was essential to my success.

Whether its a professional you can emulate, a mastermind group you can join, or a training course with a proven expert in your field, now might be the time to get a mentor in your corner.

If you're working with a single individual, it's not as simple as hitting someone up and asking them for the occasional advice about how you should run your business. Proper mentors do not go into the task lightly, and the relationship calls for a commitment and accountability on both ends. If you know someone you would like to help mentor you, you should ask them if they would do just that. They may say no, so you'll find another, or they may say yes but charge for the opportunity. If you can afford to pay, and you know this is the person you want to learn from, you should make the investment. By getting veteran experience and wisdom at your fingertips, consider how much money you will save yourself because they helped you avoid pitfalls and missed opportunities mistakes you would encounter if you went about it on your own.

Another option is a business mastermind, where small groups of people meet to commiserate and bounce ideas off each other to help everyone grow individually and collectively. Mastermind groups can be free or paid, meet regularly, and have massive amounts of accountability, but they also bring huge rewards. I know from my own experience of being in masterminds, and running my own, they can help accelerate growth in your work, but they are not to be taken lightly. Do not join one of these unless you're serious about getting some insane amounts of work done. The result will be a boatload of knowledge from both peers and experts, and fast-track movement in your business.

Training courses are the easiest barrier to entry for gathering professional knowledge, but you still must put the work in to get value out of them. Don't do the work, and you waste your time and a considerable amount of money. I had one client who, on our first conversation, told me that she had invested tens of thousands of dollars in recent years with different training programs, yet she wasn't anywhere closer to her goals than before.

The problem with training courses is that some people expect the training to be a magic pill that fixes their business without much effort on their part. If you invest in a reputable training course, you need to do the work involved, and then give it time to take effect long after the course is done.

Training courses require active participation, as well as the follow-up effort that you apply to your business. Results don't happen instantly—it's a process. Many people will take a training, fail to see immediate results, and then bounce to another training, and then another, with the only result being an emptier wallet.

Whatever route you choose, make sure you're mentally, emotionally, and physically invested in the program, otherwise you're wasting your time (and the time of others) and money. Hopefully, you're serious about your business and it's worth the time and money to help it grow. I've done all three of the above, and I can say without equivocation that they work if you invest yourself into making them work.

Challenge 15

Do you know someone in your industry who you respect and admire, and could ask for help? If so, ask them if they would be willing to mentor you to further growth. You might help them along by stating how often and for how long you would like to work with them. Also, make sure there is more benefit in it for them than for you. Perhaps that's by helping them with their work, or it's finding ways to help them share and promote their work. You could also offer to pay them for their time. Figure out some beneficial mutual ground, and then get to learning.

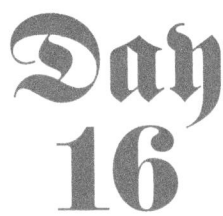

CONSIDER THE COMPANY
YOU KEEP

Author Jim Rohn said, "You are the average of the five people you spend the most time with." If you hang out with smart, sophisticated, and successful entrepreneurs, guess what happens to you. Hang out in the universe, and you become a star, but if you hang out with trash... Well, you get the point.

I love all my friends and (almost all my) family, but there are many I don't hang out with often because they do not hold the same entrepreneurial values I do. They do not share the same drive for something bigger. They're stuck in their ways of working dead-end jobs and having dead-end thoughts about dead-end things, and I don't want that to be part of my life.

I also know quite a few artists, designers, and crafters, many of them who come from a mindset of scarcity. They believe their business can only be done one way. No matter how much I try to help them grow, they will not do the work. As much as I love hanging out with creative people, some do not bring to the table the mindset I'm trying to manifest in myself.

In the past few years, I started hanging out with entrepreneurs more, and the results have been measurable. There's a mutual respect because we're all focused on our goals, even though we may be serving different markets. We share a collective spirit about the success of our individual businesses and providing tremendous value to our customers.

It's through these connections I've discovered some core principles about the people I choose to be around.

Hang Out With People You Like

Not long ago, I found myself becoming more of a shut-in. I wouldn't go so far to say I was a recluse, but I was more resistant to hanging out with people than I had been in the past. I am not sure why this happened in my late 30s, but when I took a good look at my life and how unfulfilled I was at that time, I decided to make a change. I made a pledge to be more active in my community.

I don't go out all the time. When I do, it's usually one-on-one or in very small groups, but even those get-togethers make a big difference in how I look at being social. These days, I will often jump at an invitation to hang out when people ask, even if I don't know the group that well.

Every thought leader out there will tell you that networking is one of the best things you can do for your business. Hanging out with like-minded individuals provides value in some unforeseeable ways, even if it's going out to have a good time and make new friends. Not everything has to be about business.

From my experience, many creative individuals tend to hide in their space so they can focus on their work and dwell in their comfort zone, but that can be a dangerous place, trust me. Sometimes solitude is necessary to get work done, or to recharge, but if you don't pull yourself out once in a while, you may get stuck. Next thing you know, you're Howard Hughes, growing out your fingernails and wearing tissue boxes for shoes.

Do Not Suffer Fools

On the opposite side of the spectrum, some people really suck. They will do everything in their power to hold you back, knock you down, and make you feel like trash for wanting more from life than their personal, predetermined *fair share*. Most will come at you anonymously, because it's easy, and because they can. Just read the insidious comments people leave on YouTube videos sometime.

Sadly, sometimes these people will be close friends or family members. I can almost guarantee the moment you read that last sentence, one or two names popped in your head of people like this. Am I right?

I can't tell you how many backhanded compliments I received the first week I announced I wasn't going back into the workforce but venturing out on my own instead. These *friends* think they are doing you a service by dishing out their perspective, but the truth is they are likely jealous you get to chase your dream, and they are too scared to consider the possibility for themselves.

These people don't necessarily mean you harm—they merely don't want to see you change. They like you exactly as you are, the comfortable version of you. The minute you change, you make them face the reality that *normal* is boring and lame. They're OK with boring and lame because it's safe. Their *phantom mind* has a firm grip on their psyche, and the only thing they know is how to stay safe.

Do not let these people hold you back. They do not realize true safety comes in the form of freeing yourself from the shackles of the perceived status quo. When they come at you with their comments, just smile, thank them for their input, and let it fall off you. You have no room in your life for their fears.

Sometimes they won't relent. They will come at you, knock you, or shun you. If that is the case, then perhaps the answer is to let them go. They are not one of your top five. Instead it's time to find people that encourage and embolden you.

Pick your friends and colleagues wisely. Be bold and focused about your connections, and be ready for change—it is coming. If you embrace it, it will make you even more successful.

Challenge 16

This is a three-step challenge to help improve the company you keep.

First, go through your Facebook *friends* and find people whose posts you don't really enjoy seeing in your feed. You don't have to unfriend them, but you can unfollow to keep them from crowding your feed with their posts. This doesn't mean you don't like them, just that you would rather hear from others first. Do the same for business pages that you've liked but don't need to hear from anymore.

Second, reach out to people you really appreciate hearing from—those who empower you and make you feel good when you talk to them. Let them know how much you appreciate them, and see if there is anything you can do for them. Make sure they know how much they mean to you. This will make them feel awesome, and you'll feel pretty great too.

Third, find someone you admire but don't have direct contact with. Make an effort to connect with them in some way, even if that's as simple as interacting with them regularly on their blog or in social media. Once they get a sense of who you are, and you feel like you're creating a connection, ask about connecting deeper. Maybe that's an email to show gratitude (be gracious—not creepy), or it could be a phone call. Respect their space, but don't be afraid to attempt a connection.

That last one may be scary, but do it anyway. The first time may be terrifying, but the next one will be easier, and it gets better with each new contact. Soon enough, you'll have a new circle of influences that will help improve your outlook on life.

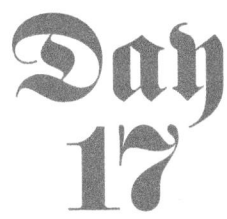

AUTHENTICITY FIRST

In a world filled with fake social media profiles and anonymous cyber-bullying, there's an abundance of space available for people who want to be honest and real online. Now is the time to fill that gap.

The word authenticity has been thrown around a lot in the past few years, and some treat it as a marketing tactic, but it doesn't have to be a cliché. The truth is, the more time you spend being your true, authentic self, the less work you have to do when someone tries to push you into a category that doesn't fit because they can only guess about what kind of person you are. Recently, I had a phone conversation with someone who is a fan of my podcast, and when we finished, she told me how much she appreciated that I was exactly as she expected me to be. This is the highest compliment anyone can give me. Not only does it make me feel good that I'm being real, but I know it makes a profound statement on the people I come in contact with when they always get me at face value.

My clients know that I can be overly generous with my time and expertise. They also know that if they try to pull some of their scripted B.S. with me, I will call them on it. I ask a lot of questions when I'm working with someone, and on many occasions, I respond to their scripted answer with, "That's bullshit!" If you're telling me a story that you've regurgitated over and over because it allows you an easy way out of tough questions, then I will call you on it. Considering that, if other people won't allow you to get away with your scripted stories about yourself, then why would you allow yourself to continue telling them?

The world wants the real you, not some homogenized, prepackaged version of you. Nobody of substance wants you to be some preordained version of yourself. We don't want you to make yourself into something you're not. If anyone does, then they are not the kind of people you should be hanging out with (Refer to yesterday's update.) If you're a brash genius with a flair for the dramatic, be that person. If you're a spitfire with a wicked sense of humor, be that. If you're a gym rat who also likes comic books and J.R.R. Tolkien, then embrace the geek level on both of those things.

I'm a big fan of classic hip-hop, and if you have listened to any in the past two decades, then you may have heard phrases like "represent", "stop frontin'", or "ain't no half-steppin'". In other words, no fakes allowed in this space! "Fake it 'til you make it," is good when you're trying to break into something new and exciting and you need to challenge yourself to rise to the occasion. It's not good when it comes to attitude and presence in the face of peers and colleagues. People will sense your false presence and maybe call you out. Then you'll be left in a lurch with a list of disenfranchised followers running for the unfollow button.

Be the person you're meant to be and your fans will love you for it. Be anything else and they will leave you behind to go find someone who will be *real* with them.

Challenge 17

This one will take guts, but don't let that stop you. Whether it's for a blog, a newsletter, or Facebook, take some time to write a post that lays out a bunch of things that people may not know about you. Make the list substantial, shooting for twenty or more items that people may be surprised to know about you. You don't have to reveal every secret, but share some new things with people that you've never shared with them.

Share your favorite items, foods, and places. Talk about your pet peeves or your quirks. Give people a small history lesson of where you've lived, where you went to school, what you studied, or what you wanted to be when you grew up. There are no rules except to share things that others don't know. Post it up and share it. If you're really brave, email me the link: dave@freshrag.com

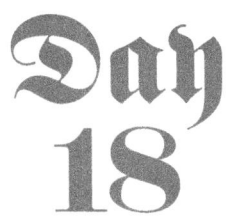

Day 18

GAUGE YOUR SUCCESS
BY *YOUR* SUCCESSES

One of the biggest problems I see with creative business owners is they gauge their progress on the success of others. Your competitors sell more than you, therefore, you must suck, right? Wrong!

Their story is not your story. Their situation has nuances that you could not reproduce no matter how hard you tried. To assume you aren't where they are because your work sucks, you are less talented, or the world hates you is a fallacy.

Instead of worrying about matching up to your competition, gauge your self-worth on your own successes. In my private mastermind group, I regularly put people on the *hot seat* to see if there are things the group can help them with in their business. The first thing I ask them to do is to call out a recent win. The win they share doesn't have to be substantial compared to others, and it may not even relate directly to their work, but it helps get them in a positive mindset about themselves. I want them to feel good about their work before we ultimately pick them apart, as I'm prone to do when they're in the hot seat. I also build them back up and congratulate their wins at the end, because often, the little things matter.

Find your wins and celebrate them. What did you do recently that was a *level-up* for you? If you finished the website you've been stressing over, rejoice. If you finally sold your first piece, celebrate that. If you got your work into a semi-prominent blog, that's a big score—capitalize on it. Stop sweating what other people do and be proud of your accomplishments. Find your own groove and stick to it, and screw what other people think.

By letting go of the burden of comparison, you free yourself up for the opportunity to grow in new and amazing ways. Following someone else's path and comparing your business to theirs limits you to a smaller range of lessons instead of the wide open prairie of wisdom that presents itself when you go for your thing.

Challenge 18

It's list-making time. Find a space where you can make a list of your wins. It can be a notebook, a chalkboard, or a post in Evernote. Where you write is less important than what you write.

Put a label at the top called BIG WINS, and once a day, or every few days, go back to your note and write down a new win. Anything that you feel good about can be a win, so don't limit yourself to definitions about what counts. Just write down the good things, and praise yourself for those things.

Later, you can look back at some of these previous wins. Some may seem silly in retrospect, because of how much you've grown, and others will remind you of why you started the work you do. The important thing is to rejoice in your accomplishments, because you should feel good about making progress.

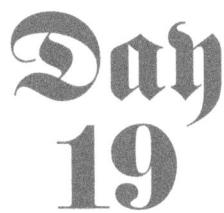

Day 19

GET OUTSIDE—GET SOME EXERCISE

Not to get all Jack Lalanne on you, but there's something to be said for anyone who lived as long as he did, looking as good as he did, right up to the end. Exercise and sunshine are two things you won't read in most business books, but the truly successful and happy individuals out there are the ones who implemented nutrition and an active lifestyle into their regimen.

It's OK if currently your idea of physical fitness is a brisk run out to the curb to take the trash out in the snow, but let's talk about endorphins for a moment. These little buggers that hang out in the pituitary gland are there, at the ready, waiting for you to call on them. Ever hear of a runner's high? Endorphins. You know that guy blasting out reps on the bench press, grunting like an animal? That happens when endorphins hang out with their buddy testosterone.

The euphoric, lightweight feeling you have after a good workout, even though you should be a crumpled mess, is your endorphins giving you a natural buzz in order to keep you from falling on your face in the parking lot. Many people don't know this feeling because they don't ever do anything active enough to kick the endorphins into action. That's a shame, because endorphins are awesome.

Another beauty of endorphins is they kickstart your energy system into high gear for hours, like drinking a Red Bull without the crash at the end. What happens when you have more energy? You're more productive and more friendly, and more people like you.

Now, endorphins don't need 300 lb. squats or 10-mile runs to kick in. The more exercise you do, the more endorphins get released, but even a brisk walk with your dog in the sun will help. Ride a bike, do some push-ups, wrestle with your kids—it's all good, and I guarantee results.

Challenge 19

This should be obvious, but go get some exercise. If you're already doing that on a regular basis, awesome! Level it up now.

If you want to make it a habit, put the time into your calendar as a date with your future hottie self. This is what I do, and it helps keep me accountable.

If it's a new thing for you, start small. Walk a few blocks one day, and then a few more. Do a mile, and then two. Stop every once in a while and do some push-ups. Keep it up and constantly try to increase your level of activity. Push a little harder, ride a little further, feel the burn, and enjoy the buzz.

One thing I've been doing lately is getting up in the morning and doing my age in push-ups. I started at 44, and as I got stronger, I added more each day. A few weeks in and I'm up over 50 push-ups each morning. Do this! It will change your life, I promise you.

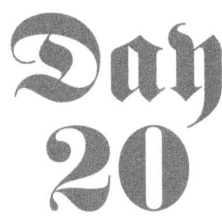

Day 20

CHAOS TAKES PRACTICE

The best part about life, and the work we do, is that there is no such thing as perfection. Yet, we are trained in our young lives to strive for perfection, even if it is unattainable. Speak when spoken to, color inside the lines, and the only good grade is an A+. I'm not sure where in time this constant strive for perfection began, but it's become a blight on the world. I believe this mindset is the cause for so many people failing to achieve their dream, because they can't get to the *perfect* result.

The way I see it, we all live our lives somewhere between complete order and total chaos. At one end of the spectrum, in complete order, lives perfection—an obvious impossibility. On the other side is total chaos, which is also an impossibility. Just as we cannot ever touch perfection, we can never devolve into total chaos. The opposing forces are constantly at battle, and at no time does one side ever relinquish control.

For an artist like myself, when I'm working, I am always fighting my own war between order and chaos. The funny thing is that depending on the work I'm doing, I find I ride that balance heavier on one side or the other. When I design graphics, I lean more toward order because design is about solving problems and communicating ideas. Order is required to maintain the legibility of the communication.

However, when I paint, I push toward chaos. I strive to run my work right to the edge of a cliff, but stop short of falling over. Sometimes I go too far with it and the piece gets scrapped, but I won't be happy with my work until I know I've taken it to the limit.

The problem with living in these two worlds is that I'm rarely doing them both at the same time. More often than not, I find myself working on design-oriented projects and, the more I do, the more order I establish within my work. This is good for communication, but I tend to get into a rut. My work becomes too orderly, and I feel stagnant. That's when I know it's time for a shift back to the art.

Recently, I started incorporating more handwritten type into my design projects, and making them as rough and distressed as possible. The problem with the work was that I'd forgotten how to be chaotic in an elegant way. The typography was either too reserved or too far over the edge to use. I went through stacks of paper trying out new styles until I finally got to a point where I felt good about the work. Now, as I put my fat, black marker down on a piece of paper, I not only have the confidence to achieve my objective, but I'm more open to where the chaotic aspects lead me. Imperfections happen all the time, but I'm learning which ones to keep and which to toss. It's not easy, but it's fun.

Yes, order and design take practice to get good, as does art and chaos. I believe that in order to become a more well-rounded creative soul, we must to live our lives in both worlds. It's a simple concept that takes a lot of work, but from my own experience, this is where true perfection lies. We will never be perfect in our work, but we can strive for balance, and in that balance, we will find a welcome home for our creativity.

Challenge 20

You already know how to work toward order and perfection. Now I want you to work toward total chaos. Whatever work you do, I want you to operate on a level of complete disorder. If you're an illustrator, work in a style that is completely unfamiliar. If you're a photographer, shoot blind. If you're a knitter, leave the pattern and color palette behind.

Work without knowing or caring about the end result. Make something with reckless abandon. Run right up to the edge of that cliff, and at the last moment, back off a step. There are no rules but to learn from your experimentation. Don't worry about wasting materials, or what you're going to do with the project when you're done. It's about the exploration, not the destination.

When you're done, make sure you share your experiments with me. Tag me on Instagram: @freshrag.

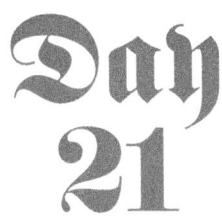

STAY THE COURSE

Back in the time of the Puritans, there was only one way to sail from England to America. They weighed the anchor, opened the sails, and pointed the bow to the West. When they set sail toward the new world, they knew it would not be a straight line from London to Plymouth Rock. They drifted in the Atlantic currents, because that's what boats do. When they drifted, the captain corrected course, and didn't stop until land was within sight. Did they find land exactly where they expected on the first attempt? Not likely, but I'm sure they were more happy to just find land instead of being cast out to sea for good.

When you're forging your way through open waters, you will drift—there is always drift—but you correct your heading and get back on course as quickly as possible. It takes a long time to cross an ocean, but the only way to get to the other side is to stay the course.

You won't see your destination until you're right up on it. It would be a shame if you traveled for weeks and weeks, only to give up early because you couldn't see the beach. Imagine if the Puritans turned around, or changed direction completely when you they were mere moments away from hearing, "Land ho." How could that have affected history?

Often I get people asking me if I can help them determine if their path is a valid one, because they don't want to go through all the work just to end up failing in the end. My typical response is that I cannot answer that question, because it is different for everyone. The only thing that separates failure from success is the effort and desire you invest in the project. You will fail, you will fall off course, and you will hit obstacles that make you challenge your beliefs, but if you're doing the work you were meant to be doing, then this should never be an issue. When failures happen, you course-correct and get back to work.

Nobody ever said pursuing a dream was easy, and if they did say it, they lied. Whatever it is you make or do, if you find yourself drifting, take a moment to find your point on the horizon, and push forward. Find your goal and aim for that. The end game is out there, and it wants you to find it, but you must stay the course.

Challenge 21

If you know your direction and you're working steadily toward your dream, then you get the day off. Celebrate your awesomeness and go do some work.

On the other hand, if you're wondering if you're heading in the right direction, stop what you're doing and take a some time to think about your goals. What is it that you want achieve with your work? What is the one thing about your work that would make you the most fulfilled? If you don't know that yet, it's time to figure it out.

When you do figure out what that thing is, then write it down and pin it to a spot on your wall so that you will see it whenever you're working. If you ever feel lost or off track, look up at that piece of paper with your goals on it, and then course-correct.

The answer may be as simple as spending less time on social media, or it could be shifting your process completely. Don't get discouraged by big changes. Embrace them because they will ultimately lead you to your goal.

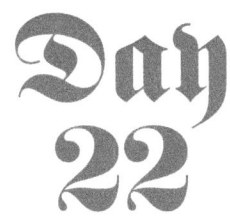

Day 22

THIS IS A MARATHON, NOT A SPRINT

Simply put, if you imagined your entire creative career as a race, would you consider yourself a sprinter or a long-distance runner? That question is rhetorical because the answer is obvious. Our business lives are not dictated by short bursts of speed that eventually get us to our goal, but that's exactly how some people treat their work.

Some creative folk believe that to take advantage of every opportunity, they need to rush into projects, extract what they can from them, and when it doesn't pan out right away, move into something else. Literally every single day I see people talking about the next big thing they want to do with their business long before they've realized their full potential on what they are doing now. A fine artist wants to make prints, and then posters, and then cards, and then products. A knitter wants to make scarves, and then hats, and then patterns for others. A photographer wants to take photos of street life, and then nature, and then people, and then animals.

It's perfectly OK to continue pushing your work until you find your muse. Experiment with new methods, genres, and mediums, but don't chase them all, thinking that the next one is going to lead you to your untapped success. Instead, find your thing, and work that thing for all it's worth. The goal should be to become the best, or best known, for that thing that only you do. Do your thing, do it well, and do it consistently. Share every single aspect of your work in a way that only you can because nobody else does that thing like you.

It takes time to be that person who does your thing like nobody else. It takes a LOT of time. Get used to that idea, and own it. Over time, your work may shift as your inspiration changes, but it should be a natural progression of the work. Forcing yourself into new areas, because you think *that* is where your success lies, only gets you further away from your expertise.

I'm sure you've heard the idiom, "Jack of all trades, master of none." In a world where the competition for attention is getting stiffer each day, the way to set yourself apart from the rest of the world is to become the craftsman only you can be. The *all things to all people* approach does not work anymore. Instead, be the best of that one thing, to the people who matter, for years to come.

Challenge 22

If you're spread too thin, focusing your energy in several directions at once, then maybe it's time to cull the herd a bit. If you're working really hard to maintain a bunch of different projects or product lines, but not getting any further along, then you might be in need of some trimming.

Take a long, hard look at all the things you are doing in your work. Force yourself to eliminate aspects of your work that 1) don't bring you any joy, and 2) don't make you money.

Next, focus on the things you do that bring you joy, but don't bring much return (money, fans, awareness). What can you do to improve those elements so they become more viable? Can you share more, market more, or make them better? If the answer is no, or it would be too time-consuming, then maybe those items need to go on the back burner until you're ready to spend more time on them.

What you're left with are the things that bring you joy and make you money. It doesn't have to be a lot of money, but enough to build on and improve. Focus your time, energy, and marketing on making those items the best they can be. Become the champion for those joyful money makers. When they become so popular that they almost sell themselves, then consider bringing in new items, but not before then.

Good luck, and remember, be honest, brutal, and relentless.

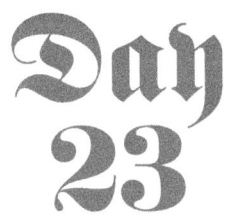

Day 23

SHARE YOUR AWESOME

This one may seem simple, but it's more in-depth than posting pictures of your stuff on Instagram and Pinterest. Yes, do that, often. However, the manner in which you share will distinguish you from your competition, even if they do it on the same platforms.

Some of you will not agree with what I'm about to tell you. Some will think I'm taking this a bit far, getting too personal, but I'm telling you now, this works if you let it. Instead of just posting a photo with an obscure title and a link to where they can find it, maybe try writing a blog post about the thought process behind the work. Consider telling a personal story that got you to create the piece. Then share it on your social networks with an intriguing title that piques interest on a personal level.

You see, your customers, clients, and followers want to know more about you. They don't have to know everything, but the more humanity you share, the more they will love you. I have wrestled with the idea of sharing pics of my son on my various accounts, because I don't want to put him at undue risk or exploit him, but I share because it gives context to my life beyond the words I write or the art I create. Plus, I know people like my kid. What can I say, he's freakin' cute.

All bias aside, the stories I share about my family are the ones people resonate with most. No longer is my story just about being an artist, designer, and media strategist, but I'm also a husband and father who works to make a better life for his family. That story alone has brought so many people to me I can't even count them. Here's the thing, though, none of it is contrived. Every post I share is authentic. I regularly share pics of my kid with people because I love him and I love bragging about him. I'd share pics in line at the coffee shop as soon as I would on Twitter. It's organic and real, and that is why people appreciate it. Plus, the aforementioned cuteness, of course.

I'm not saying everyone should share pics of their kids, their family, or anything personal, but figure out where your personal limits are, and then share something that lets people know you're human.

It doesn't have to be pictures, either. It could be written words in a blog post telling a personal story that relates to your work in some way. It could be a video diary where you express your thoughts and interests, or an audio recording posted to Soundcloud.

The manner in which you share is not important, but rather, that you share at all. Put yourself out there and people will resonate and commiserate with you. The old days of only posting random links to your work, hoping people click through, won't cut it anymore. Your fans don't want a mythical entity with no personality who exists behind some cropped profile pic. They want you. Tell a story and share <u>you</u> with them.

Challenge 23

Time to dig deep. Share something personal with your fans in a way that is unfamiliar. You don't have to do this all the time, but sharing the more intimate sides of your life will bring more people to your circle of influence.

Write a blog post, post something on your Facebook page, share photos on Instagram, or be open and honest with your newsletter subscribers. Where and how does not matter, as long as you do it.

When you share, share it with me. Tag me in whichever social media outlet you choose. Again, @freshrag pretty much everywhere.

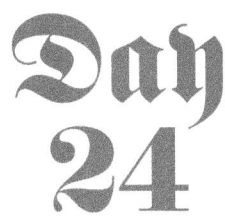

Day 24

NOT A MISTAKE, BUT A MISSED TAKE

We've all seen those moments in television and movies where they dramatize the process of shooting a film or show. They show actors going through a scene over and over until they get just the right feel the director is looking for in that scene. My favorite is from David Lynch's Mulholland Drive, where Naomi Watts goes in for a screen test with another actor. The first scene plays out fairly well but lacks real heart. The director calls "cut," gives a slight bit of direction to the male actor, and they play the scene again. The second attempt is steamy, smoldering even, and completely changes the scene despite being the same words spoken.

Not all second takes in the movies come out quite so dramatic, but they always happen. Second, third, tenth, and thirtieth takes happen on a regular basis. This is considered the norm. It's how they do business.

I bring this up to illustrate that life is filled with second takes, and they happen to everyone. Yet, some of us will try something new, and when it doesn't work the first time, we give up. In the past, I was the king of this, but I have since learned my lesson. Can you imagine if a Stephen Spielberg took all the time, energy, and money to put a production together, and after the first failed take, his threw up his hands and walked away from the set?

If we reframe our outlook, and think of *failures* instead as new opportunities to learn, then we improve our chance of success. Instead of treating failure as a mistake, think of it as a missed take. That last take didn't work, so we go again, and we keep going until we get it to work, or we find a new way to look at the work we're doing.

Life is rarely filled with first-take successes. You may have had one or two, but I'm going to guess you've had far more second and third takes. However, we get idealistic about our first-take moments, imagining that we can hit our cues perfectly each time. That is unrealistic and detrimental. In fact, it's possible that some of your first-take moments could have been improved with a second or third approach to them.

Embrace your second, third, and other opportunities to learn and improve upon the work. It will keep your momentum headed in the right direction, and make you better at what you do.

Challenge 24

Think back to the last time you ran into a wall with your work, or you had what you considered a failure, and you tossed that work aside. If you haven't had that moment, congratulations—you're one of the few who learned early on to embrace *missed takes*.

If you did have one of those moments, take some time to consider what you could have done different that would have kept your momentum going forward, and where you might be now if you had pushed through until success.

One caveat: Do not dwell. It's good to look back and learn from missed takes, but don't ponder them too long. Don't get down on yourself because you can see where you'd be if you had pushed through. That will do you no good at all. You can't change that path anymore than you can call on the rain. Instead, learn from it, and apply what you learn to future missed takes.

If you want to take it a bit further, share your story about the missed take and how you will do things different if you run into that situation again. Post on your blog, Facebook, or Medium, and then share it with me. I can't wait to read about your future success.

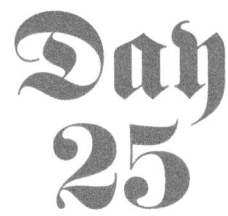

Day 25

REWARD YOURSELF

Work-life balance can seem like an impossible goal, but I would be remiss if I didn't remind you to take time to enjoy life away from your studio or office. There will always be time for work, but not always time to do the things you may regret missing out on later.

One thing veteran entrepreneurs understand is the relationship between time and money. They know that there will always be opportunities to make more money, but you can't get more time, so use it to your advantage. Go ahead and make your money, but not at the expense of making memories.

I don't have many regrets in life, but one of my biggest is that I didn't travel more when I was younger. I went through life making listless decisions about my direction, and I never understood the value of travel. Now that I have a family, a mortgage, and other domestic responsibilities, it's a lot tougher for me to take off for parts unknown. When I do, I make sure to value that time.

With family as a priority, I skip trips and work more often. I do this to provide. However, I've learned that watching my son grow up is my most important job, and my biggest reward for all the hard work I put in. I spend a little bit of each day watching this tiny creature turn into a well-adjusted human, and it is by far the best gift I could give myself. I'm making these memories now because there may not be an opportunity later.

When you're working away at whatever project you have cooking, make sure you reflect on the reasons why you're putting that work in. Don't wait for some elusive moment when you can stop working and enjoy life. Go enjoy life in the micro-moments you have available now. The work will still be there when you get back.

Challenge 25

Stop working, close your computer, and go do something that creates a memory. Maybe that's a phone call to an old friend, a walk in the park with your spouse, or some alone time with a good book. Take a drive to somewhere new, enjoy a new dish for dinner, or play with your kids. No kidding, as soon as I finish this section, I'm goign to close my computer, and go hang out with my son, because that is far more important that finishing this book.

Whether you hang out with family, or spend time with yourself in solitude, go do that thing, and be ok with letting the work sit for awhile. It doesn't matter what you do, as long as you respect and enjoy the time spent.

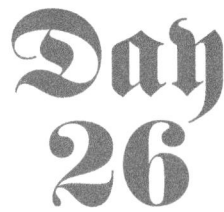

Day 26

FORGIVENESS IS FREEING

WARNING: I'm about to get really deep into a personal story.

It feels like it was yesterday. I was maybe 3 or 4 years old, and I was playing in the park with my dad. I don't recall all the details, of course, but I do remember that I hadn't seen him in a while. After a bit of playing, my mom collected me and told me to say goodbye to him. He told me he wasn't going to be around much anymore, and I remember losing my mind over it.

I don't recall how long it took me to grasp the reality of the situation, but I do remember holding a torch for his return. It was so strong that no matter who my mother got involved with after, they were my enemy. I hated them before I knew them. I can't say I consciously sabotaged her relationships with other men, but I'm sure there was a little of that happening subconsciously.

I did get to see my father over time. We maintained a relationship via phone calls, but because he moved to a different state I only got to see him in the summer months. As a kid, I held him in high regard, despite my deep-seated feelings. He and my bother had a contentious post-wed relationship, but I treated him like a hero.

Over the years, my father had been in and out of my life, and I gave him plenty of opportunity to take advantage of my emotions. Several times he disappeared without any word. I had to learn his whereabouts from other family members, and I was usually the one who had to rekindle the relationship. Finally, in my 30s, he made a move to distance himself from me again, but this time I'd had enough. I was one that told him that I would no longer burden him with his fatherly duties. It was liberating, but strangely unfulfilling.

I was angry for a few years after that. I would dream about what I would do if I ever saw him again, and there were many violent thoughts. It was a very dark time in my life, and I made a lot of other people unhappy because of my feelings toward my father.

One day, after having a venomous conversation with my mother, she said something about my father, and even though I seethed at the mere mention of him, I felt compelled to defend him. Old habits die hard, I guess. However, in that moment, I knew I needed to fix something. I didn't know what it was, but I needed to do something.

I remember reading some blog posts about getting past unhealthy relationships, and the pervasive lesson I picked up on was that I needed to forgive him for the way he treated me all my life. It sounded insane to me, because the last thing I wanted was to talk to him ever again. I worried that he would try to manipulate me again, and I didn't want to give him that opportunity. Considering my options, I decided to write him an email expressing all my feelings and letting him know how I felt, but that I forgave him for the past.

It was the longest email I had ever written, and I wasn't even sure he would have the attention to read something that long. Instead of sending it, though, I let it sit in my draft folder for a long time, but something miraculous happened. I felt better.

The thing I have realized about forgiveness is that it's more for me than it is for him. By forgiving him, I am letting loose the chains of anger and sadness that weighed me down. I am opening myself up to the possibility of love for others when I let go of the hate I had for him. I forgave him for *my* freedom, not his.

Instead of sending that email to him, I sent it to myself, and then I archived it for future access. My anger toward him was a bit of an addiction, and just because I forgave him that one time, that does not mean the anger went away forever. When those old feelings come bubbling back up, I remind myself that he no longer has the control. I took back the control with my forgiveness. It's an ongoing process, but it works for me. In fact, just writing about it now makes me feel better about myself.

The lesson should be obvious, but if you're holding onto any anger, sadness, or regret over something that happened between you and a family member or friend, then maybe now is the time to forgive them. You may not realize it, but the feelings you keep stored up are having an effect on you and the people around you. It might not be as intense as my anger, but it is making a difference. If you relinquish those feelings in favor of forgiveness, you open yourself up to love and happiness. You take back control, and you can then lead a more fruitful and productive life.

Challenge 26

If there is someone in your life you've harbored bad feelings toward because of how they treated you, consider forgiveness. Write them a letter or email and tell them exactly how you feel, and that you are ready to let go of it. This does not mean you have to maintain a relationship with them—I still do not talk to my dad—but you get to move on and have better feelings about the situation.

Write the email or letter and hold onto it until you're ready to send it. That may be right away, or it may be never. But remember, it's not about their absolution, but your happiness. You're writing for you, not them. It's time to let loose the chains.

As a cautionary note, when you write that letter, perhaps don't fill out the "to:" field, just in case you hit the send button out of habit. Accidents happen, right?

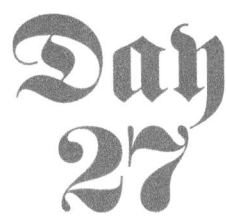

WHEN TO SAY YES—WHEN TO SAY NO

Many times throughout our day, we are forced to make decisions about what we are going to do with our precious time. Work or play? Shower or grunge? Eat or work out? Make or promote? Hang out with friends or stay home?

Every single day is filled with these decisions. Sometimes we make them without thinking, and other times our choices are deliberate, but how often are you making the right decision? The unfortunate part is that we may not know the answer until we've already committed to one decision or the other. Have you ever gone to a party or meet-up and realized once you were there that it was a complete waste of time? Your friends didn't show, and the people you're hanging out with aren't your kind of people? You can't help but think to yourself, "I should have stayed home and saved the gas."

Other times you may be faced with a decision to join in on something cool, but you decide against it because the outcome is uncertain. You choose to not go because you're not sure you'll enjoy yourself, but find out later it was the best thing to happen to the people who participated.

We experience these moments all the time, and because of their frequency, we are complacent to acknowledge them as potential turning points in our life, whether we say yes, or no.

This reminds me of the spring of 2014. My ten-year wedding anniversary was approaching, and my wife and I had originally planned to go back to Hawaii, the place where we got married. One day, my wife said she wanted to go to Europe instead and visit her sister and family. Up until this moment, I felt a bit xenophobic to Europe, and I didn't really see the need to go there because Hawaii sounded so much better. Knowing how much it meant to my wife, I said yes to her idea, and it was the best decision of my life.

Of course it was a good decision because I wanted to keep being married to my wife, and she would not have been pleased had I said no. Also, it was a wise decision because Europe (Paris, more specifically) ended up being incredibly inspirational for me. It was the creative shot in the arm that I had been yearning for but didn't know I needed until that moment. Now instead of yearning to go back to Hawaii, I'm more inclined to head back to Europe. In fact, I encourage every single person reading this book to visit Paris one time in your life, because it will change your world, especially if you're an artist.

Not all yes/no situations are as profound as a trip to Europe, but they may have lasting effects on us nonetheless. How do we figure out which ones we should indulge, and which ones should we pass on? The best way I know is to ask yourself how the decision will affect your life, no matter how small the effect.

Before you answer any yes/no question, remember to ask yourself one other question first: Does this decision get me closer to or further from my goal? Meaning, if you're trying to focus your energy to finish a series of work, does going to a party make the most sense? If you're trying to keep your head down and knock out work, then no, but if you're feeling some burnout and need a release, then perhaps yes. Does it make sense to say yes to an acquaintance who wants to buy you coffee and pick your brain about the work you do? Or would it be better to say no until a later time?

If you know the goal you're trying to achieve, and you address a situation by asking if that decision supports your goal or not, then you're on your way to more productivity. Sometimes a party is a good idea, and sometimes not so much. Coffee with an acquaintance my be a good plan, or it may be a complete time suck. The decision will always be best determined by examining your goals first, and then making your choice.

Challenge 27

This challenge is a bit hypothetical, because it requires the actions of others, so you may not be able to do it right away, but keep it in the front pocket of your mind when a yes/no decision arises.

Next time someone asks you to hang out, or they want to pick your brain, ask if the choice gets you to your goal, or keeps you away from it a little longer. The decision will not always be clear, but the more often you ask yourself the question, the more clear things become.

PS - Hawaii and coffee are always a good idea, especially if you can do them together. Just sayin'.

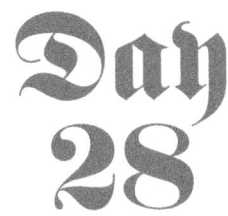

TAKE ACTION

You made it! You finished the *Creative Badass Challenge*, and that is so freaking rad. If you made it to this page, I am proud and stoked for you, but you're not quite out of the woods yet.

As we wrap this challenge, there is one last piece of advice I need to hand over. Whatever it is you're starting, do it now. Do not wait for the right time, right place, right audience. Those things never come in a timely fashion, and often don't come at all.

Done is better than perfect, because perfect does not exist. If you wait for work to be perfect, you will never finish, or you will finish late and miss the reward because someone beat you to market.

While they percolate in your brain, your ideas can appear big and beautiful, but unless you take action, they mean nothing. Remember that there is no such thing as perfect, so taking action today gets you closer to your goal sooner.

Steve Jobs said, "Real artists ship," which means put your work out now, even unfinished—test and tune later. This is commonly referred to as a minimum viable product, and it means putting something out that people can appreciate and get value from, while you ask for feedback, and then tweak the product to make it better. Your work might have problems, might be only 95% done, but the important factor is that you got it out there.

Your level of success depends on how quickly you can take action. The faster you move, the quicker you get to start counting dollar bills. Hesitate, and you may let those dollars slip through your fingers and into the hands of your competition.

Whatever it is you need to do for your business—start a blog, find a new supplier, make new products, hire an employee—start that thing today and get moving. You don't have to finish today, but you must start now if you want to see success sooner.

Remember, inaction leads to complacency. Complacency leads to inertia, and inertia becomes death to all your big ideas. Do not let your inaction today kill tomorrow's dreams. Make them happen, and take action now.

Challenge 28

I have two tasks for you on this final day. First, I want you to share with the world that you finished the challenge and you are an official Creative Badass. You now have the tools to own your awesome whenever you need.

Second: Use those tools, and never let them go. Like any craftsman, the more you use the tools, the better you get at them. To become a Creative Badass master, you must use the tools daily, throughout your life. They don't hand out black belts for creative badassery, but if they did, it would only happen after decades of application. Do the work.

I hope you've enjoyed this journey and you got some great value from it. If you did enjoy it, and you know others who might also appreciate it, send them over to CreativeBadassChallenge.com.

Finally, I want to know how this challenge affected your life and your work. Please make sure you email me and tell me your story. Also, if you have questions about anything in this book, feel free to email me direct: dave@freshrag.com.

Thanks again for being a participant in the journey. I can't wait to hear about what life has in store for you in the future. Best of luck, and if you need help, you know where to reach me.

Appendix

EXTRA GOODIES TO MAKE YOUR JOURNEY BETTER

GET THE WORKBOOK

If you feel like you didn't get enough work out of this challenge, I've got some more homework for you. It's called the *Creative Badass Workbook*, and it gives you multiple new opportunities to make some cool stuff happen, each coordinated with the various challenges. If you are that kind of overachiever, then have I got a book for you.

http://bit.ly/cbcworkbook

Videos

Each day's challenge comes with a special video that coincides with the content of the day, but adds a little extra oomph. Have a look, and enjoy.

WELCOME
http://youtu.be/NO02uMrfxx8

PREGAME
http://youtu.be/iLJCIuNc_M0

DAY 1
http://youtu.be/alX2ZB7ze28

DAY 2
http://youtu.be/1bzlESsTU6E

DAY 3
https://youtu.be/EkE44g7MspQ

DAY 4
http://youtu.be/ELHc_6IHZIc

DAY 5
http://youtu.be/Du9G2n-lrV4

DAY 6
http://youtu.be/UGfz_sYrAVI

DAY 7
http://youtu.be/Od-UMWvctzk

DAY 8
http://youtu.be/UbknAdb8eZM

DAY 9
http://youtu.be/xeoyoOnROE4

DAY 10
http://youtu.be/4e8LVrpfLok

DAY 11
http://youtu.be/QjTnoLXfxAE

DAY 12
http://youtu.be/1yKYBm9UhWg

DAY 13
http://youtu.be/YDAkr3rpFBA

DAY 14
http://youtu.be/hbhXcuRByY0

DAY 15
http://youtu.be/HaecPISWD6Q

DAY 16
http://youtu.be/4qCR1fuapVI

DAY 17
http://youtu.be/0Mxjh2bat2Q

DAY 18
http://youtu.be/r8YQ-1zatpM

DAY 19
http://youtu.be/_kDJwAwfadQ

DAY 20
http://youtu.be/B1eU4aaHgAk

DAY 21
http://youtu.be/sPhavjOVOFw

DAY 22
http://youtu.be/KVuT14-g7k8

DAY 23
http://youtu.be/rYXFo-PS5gs

DAY 24
http://youtu.be/0LqqmQiDxgQ

DAY 25
http://youtu.be/6n_lfE-Kf-s

DAY 26
http://youtu.be/MhKkHxZmqfk

DAY 27
http://youtu.be/_t2yQTA3FK4

DAY 28
http://youtu.be/-bKTGku_SKM

Audio

Prefer audio instead? I took all the videos and turned them into MP3 files for you to download for your listening pleasure. I can't promise I won't break your ear drums from the shouting, though.

DAY 0 TO 7
http://bit.ly/cbcaudio1

DAY 8 TO 14
http://bit.ly/cbcaudio2

DAY 15 TO 21
http://bit.ly/cbcaudio3

DAY 22 TO 28
http://bit.ly/cbcaudio4

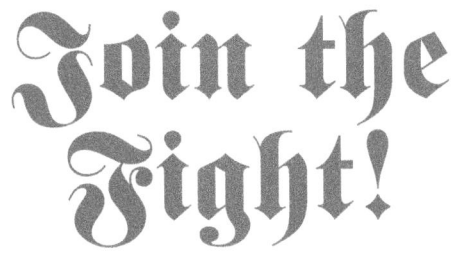

Join the Fight!

DO GOOD THINGS WITH OTHERS

I've opened up a private Facebook group specifically for creative badasses like you. I call it The Fresh Rag Army, and I want to recruit you to join the ranks.

www.freshrag.com/army

If you haven't signed up for the Fresh Rag News, you should get on that. It's free and I'm dropping new information in a weekly basis, so of which is so golden, you'd be crazy to not get it. However, it's only for subscribers. There's also a free ebook or two in it for you if you sign up today.

www.freshrag.com/news

Can't get enough Dave in your life? How about having me direct into your eardrums each week? *The Fresh Rag Show* is a weekly (or more) podcast where I sit down with today's most compelling creatives to share their stories and insights. These conversations are not to be missed.

www.freshrag.com/theshow

Can I Ask a Favor?

THIS WOULD HELP ME OUT A BUNCH

As a self-published author, I thrive on three things. First is sales (big surprise), second is referrals (share this with someone, would ya?), and third is ratings on Amazon.

It is my goal to provide so much value, you can't help but do great things with your business. At the very end of this book, you will have an opportunity to rate my effort and share your thoughts with the community. I want you to voice your opinions without falter, and I appreciate any thoughts you may have about what you read, so please share. Even slightly, unfavorable ratings are better than no ratings, so I welcome whatever you have to share.

That said, I hope you give it top marks, because that would be awesome. If you did enjoy it, please share it with your friends and family. Hopefully, we can keep this ball rolling, and change the landscape of how creative business owners treat themselves and their businesses. *Vive le créatif révolucion.*

www.freshrag.com/rate-cbc

Also by Dave Conrey

SELLING ART ONLINE

Your art deserves to be seen! If you're an artist, designer, illustrator, or photographer, Selling Art Online will help you find ways to get your art into the hands of more people. It's a comprehensive look at various platforms where you can share your work, as well as business fundamentals for taking your work to the next level.

www.freshrag.com/sao

LIFE AFTER CHRISTMAS

The key to a successful creative business these days starts with consistent branding, and consistent branding begins with quality storytelling that engages and enlists new fans and followers. If you're not doing the work to attract the exact right kind of people to your business, you may be wasting time and energy. Life After Christmas is all about helping you find that delicate balance between a business owner and a human being.

www.freshrag.com/lac

THE GOLD IS IN THE LIST

I've already talked about the virtues of starting and maintaining a healthy email list. Well, I finally put all my knowledge on the subject into a handy guide to get you started. This book vows to help get you to your first 1,000 subscribers and beyond, and if you follow the strategy, it will be the best investment you can make in your marketing efforts.

www.freshrag.com/gold

About the Author

Dave Conrey is an author, artist, and podcaster. When not spending time playing dinosaurs and robots with his son, he is working on a number of creative projects, ranting on his podcast, or writing his next book.

Before launching his own brand, he worked for two decades as a marketing professional and art director, and he uses this experience to inform, engage, and advise creative entrepreneurs on how to take their work from a hobby to a viable business. Visit daveconrey.com to get updates on everything he is working on.

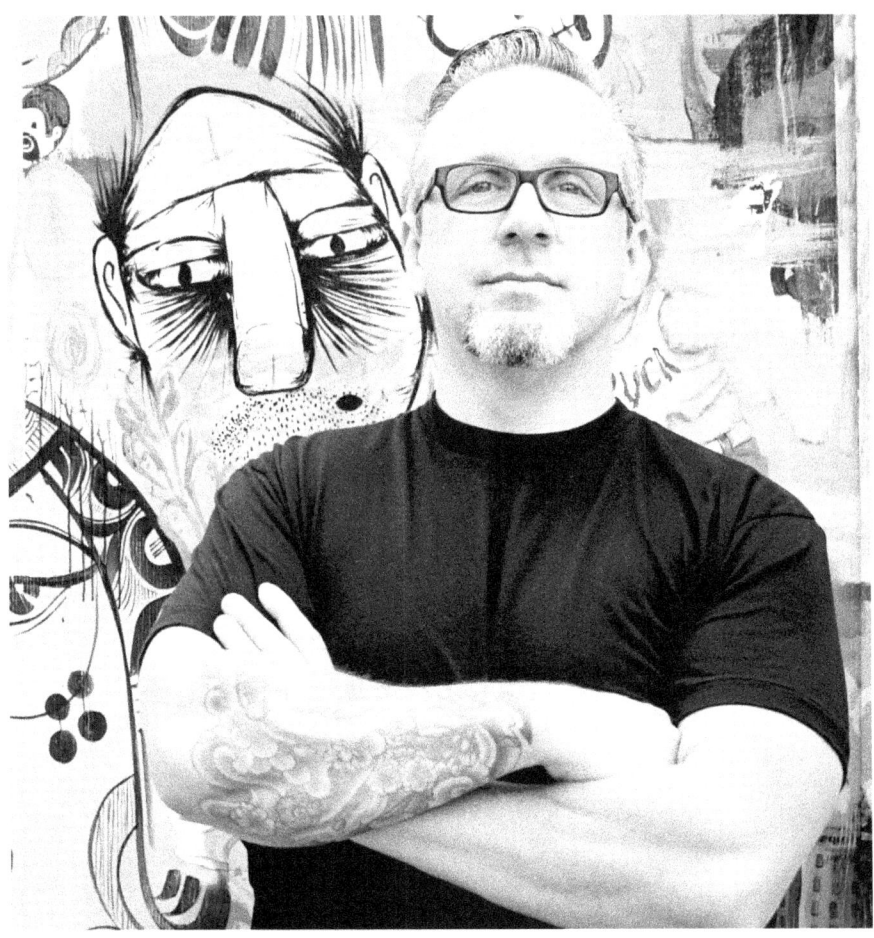

CREATIVE
BADASS
Challenge